How To Read

Emoji Books combine words and emojis together to tell a story. One Emoji means a single word and two or more Emojis can mean one or more words:

🤷 = I don't know

🎊🎂 = Happy Birthday

If you need help, you can always check out the Legend in the back of this book. It will help you understand what the Emojis in the story mean.

Enjoy!

It was a Thursday afternoon at 🏫, and Tommie was in math class, his least favorite subject. Just before the 🔔 🔊, the 👨‍🏫 began telling the class that there will be a big test tomorrow on everything that they had learned. Tommie was 🙁. He was doing well on his homework and had been paying attention when the 👨‍🏫 was giving his lessons, but he was still getting a 🅒 in class.

The next morning when Tommie woke up to get ready for 🏫, he was still 😟 about the big math test that day. He didn't want to fail the test because he knew his grades would only get worse. He 🙏 that there were a way that he didn't have to take the test. Then, Tommie had an 💡.

"👩‍👦!" Tommie 🗣. "I don't feel too good."

Tommie's 👩 was in the other room getting ready for work.

"Oh, 🍯. Are you 🤒?" she asked.

"Ye-Yes," Tommie said nervously.

"Okay, 🍯. Just stay in 🛏 and rest. I have to

go to work, but I should be back around 3️⃣ 🕒. I'll make you some 🍵. It will be in the kitchen."

"Thanks, 👩," Tommie said. He didn't like lying to his 👩, but he knew that if he went to 🏫, he would fail that test for sure.

After Tommie's 👩‍🦰 finished making the 🍵, she left to go to work. Tommie got out of 🛏️ and 👀 out of the 🪟 to make sure she was gone.

"Well, I'm not going to 🏠, and 👩‍🦰 is going to be gone for a while.

What am I going to do?" Tommie 🤔 to himself.

"Let's 👀 what's on 📺."

Tommie turned on the 📺 and 👀 through all of the channels, but he couldn't find anything to 👀. The cartoons he liked to 👀 didn't come on until after he was 🏡 from 🏫. This day was not starting off well.

Tommie went to the kitchen to eat his breakfast. After he was done eating, he 🤔 of another 💡.

"I know! I'll just play some 🎮📺. That will help pass the time."

Tommie 🏃 upstairs to his room and was getting ready to grab the 🎮 when he 👂 the front 🚪 open.

"Tom Tom!?" he 👂 a

lady say. It was Ms. Peterson, their next-🚪 neighbor.

"Your 👩‍🍼 called me and said you were 🤒, so I came over to check on you."

Tommie dropped the 🎮 and jumped into 🛏️ as

quick as he could.

"I'm in my room, Mrs. Peterson!" Tommie 🗣️ back.

"Oh, okay dear, I'll be in and out today to make sure you're all right. Try and get some 😴."

"Great," Tommie 🤔.

How was he supposed to play 🎮📺 with Ms. Peterson checking in on him? If she 👂 the 📺 on, she's going to find out that Tommie really isn't 🤒.

"Maybe I can still play with my toys and be really 🤫," Tommie 🤔. Tommie brought out his action figures and began playing with them. Tommie was finally starting to have fun staying 🌳🏠 from 🏫. He was ready to take more toys out when he 👂 the front 🚪 open again.

"Tom-Tom!" It was Ms. Peterson again.

"I'm going to be in the backyard checking on your 👩's garden. She really needs to take these weeds out. After I'm done, I'll warm you up some 🍵 to eat."

Tommie couldn't believe it. Now Ms. Peterson was going to stay at his 🏡 for the rest of the day. There was no way he could play in his room without her knowing that he wasn't in 🛏️.

After Ms. Peterson finished working in the garden, she warmed up the 🍵 Tommie's 👩‍👦 made for him.

"Now after you finish eating, I want you to go back to 🛏, so you can get better. Okay?"

"Yes, ma'am," Tommie said 🥺.

Tommie had nothing else to do besides going to 😴, so he did.

Tommie woke up a while later to the 🔊 of his 👩‍👦 coming 🏡 from work. She thanked Ms. Peterson for helping out around the 🏡 and went upstairs to check on Tommie.

"How are you feeling, 🍯?" his 👩‍👦 asked.

Tommie felt really bad. Not only did he lie to his 👩‍🍼 about being 🤒, but he didn't have any fun staying 🏡 from 🏫 either.

"👩‍🍼, there's something I have to tell you."

"What is it, 🍯?" his 👩‍🍼 asked 😟.

"There was a big math test today at 🏫 that I knew I was going to fail. I was so 🙁 about it that I decided to pretend to be 🤒 so I wouldn't have to go."

"I 👀. Was it worth it?" his 👩 asked.

"No. I couldn't do anything. There was nothing on 📺, and Ms. Peterson kept checking on me, so I had to go to 😪 the entire day. I'm really sorry I lied to you. I won't do it again." Tommie said.

"🍯, there are going to be things that will scare you or 🙁 you about failing. You're not going to get past them by running away and even worse, lying. The best thing to do is to face them head on, even if you know you're going to fail. Because if you don't even try, you have failed already."

"You're right, 👩‍👦, the next time I'm 🙁 about a test, I'll just study as hard as I can and take it anyway."

"That's good, 🍯. Because I'm going to 📞 your 👨‍🏫 and make sure that he gives you that test on Monday! You're going to study all weekend for it, and you're not going outside or playing with any of your toys until then."

Tommie should have known that was coming.

"Okay 👩‍👦," Tommie said disappointed.

Tommie spent all weekend studying for his math test. He learned that you can't 🏃 from your problems and that the best thing to do is to face them. He also learned that lying is never a good thing to do and promised Ms. Peterson that he would help her with whatever she needed to make up for it.

The End

Legend

1. 🏫 - School
2. 🔔 🔊 - Bell Rang
3. 👨‍🏫 - Teacher
4. 😟 - Worried
5. 👨‍🏫 - Teacher
6. 🆗 - C
7. 🏫 - School
8. 😟 - Worried
9. 🙏 - Wished

10. 💡 - Idea

11. 👩‍👦 - Mom

12. 🗣️ - Yelled

13. 👩‍👦 - Mom

14. 🍯 - Honey

15. 🤒 - Sick

16. 🍯 - Honey

17. 🛏️ - Bed

18. 3️⃣ 🕒 - 3 O'clock

19. 🍵 - Soup

20/21. 👩‍👦 - Mom

22. 🏫 - School
23. 👩‍👦 - Mom
24. 🍵 - Soup
25. 🛏️ - Bed
26. 👀 - Looked
27. 🪟 - Window
28. 🏫 - School
29. 👩‍👦 - Mom
30. 🤔 - Thought
31. 👀 - See
32/33. 📺 - TV

34/35/36. 👀 - Looked/Watch/Watch

37. 🏡 - Home

38. 🏫 - School

39. 🤔 - Thought

40. 💡 - Idea

41. 🎮📺 - Video Games

42. 🏃 - Ran

43. 🎮 - Controller

44. 👂 - Heard

45. 🚪 - Door
46. 👂 - Heard
47. 🚪 - Door
48. 👩‍👦 - Mom
49. 🤒 - Sick
50. 🎮 - Controller
51. 🛏️ - Bed
52. 🗣️ - Yelled
53. 😴 - Sleep
54. 🤔 - Thought

55. 🎮📺 - Video Games

56. 👂 - Heard

57. 📺 - TV

58. 🤒 - Sick

59. 🤫 - Quiet

60. 🤔 - Thought

61. 🏡 - Home

62. 🏫 - School

63. 👂 - Heard

64. 🚪 - Door

65. 👩‍👦 - Mom

66. 🍵 - Soup

67. 🏡 - House

68. 🛏️ - Bed

69. 🍵 - Soup

70. 👩‍👦 - Mom

71. 🛏️ - Bed

72. 🥺 - Sadly

73. 😴 - Sleep

74. 🔊 - Sound

75. 👩‍👦 - Mom

76/77. 🏡 - Home

78. 🍯 - Honey

79/80. 👩‍👦 - Mom

81. 🤒 - Sick

82. 🏡 - Home

83. 🏫 - School

84. 👩‍👦 - Mom

85. 🍯 - Honey

86. 👩‍👦 - Mom

87. 😟 - Worried

88. 🏫 - School

89. 😟 - Worried

90. 🤒 - Sick

91. 👀 - See

92. 👩‍👦 - Mom

93. 📺 - TV

94. 😴 - Sleep

95. 🍯 - Honey

96. 😟 - Worried

97. 🏃 - Running

98. 👩‍👦 - Mom

99. 😟 - Worried

100. 🍯 - Honey

101. 📞 - Call

102. 👨‍🏫 - Teacher

103. 👩‍👦 - Mom

104. 🏃 - Run

Printed in Great Britain
by Amazon